The Roof of the World

Between the wind-swept plateaux of Tibet and the deep mountain valleys of Nepal is the 'roof of the world'. Here rise the Himalaya Mountains – the 'land of the snows'. And towering above all the mighty Himalayan peaks stands Mount Everest, at 8848 metres the highest point on earth.

Where Everest now soars above the clouds there was once a great sea. The mountains were formed between 7 and 25 million years ago, as the Indian sub-continent moved northwards to collide with Tibet. The Himalayas are still rising, as the rocks beneath the Earth are forced upwards by the colossal pressure.

Snow and ice cover the rocky slopes and slow-moving glaciers grind their way down into distant valleys. Only in these valleys can plants and animals survive the extremes of the climate.

In the Khumbu Valley, in the shadow of Everest, live the Sherpas. These mountain people are used to the demands of altitude. They provide invaluable help to climbers such as Edmund Hillary by acting as guides and porters. The Sherpas can follow the twisting mountain tracks for many hours without tiring. They grow crops of potatoes and corn and keep herds of yaks. Yaks are the mountain cattle of the Himalayas.

The Sherpas are Buddhists. And high in the mountains travellers are welcomed at lonely monasteries, where prayer wheels spin endlessly in the wind and prayer flags flutter on tall poles.

Hillary and his fellow climbers were entertained by Sherpa stories of the yeti, a mysterious creature said to look like a large hairy ape. But its existence has never been proved.

Sherpa houses nestle close together in the valleys and are surrounded by tiny terraced fields. Yaks and snow leopards are protected by their thick coats against the intense cold.

Chomolungma

Before the 1850s the Himalayas were almost unknown to the outside world. Few Europeans had ever made the long and difficult journey to Tibet and Nepal hidden beyond their wall of mountains.

At this time India was part of the British Empire. And the British government was anxious to know exactly how large India was. The man given this task was the Surveyor-General, George Everest.

A survey team travelled across India, using trigonometry to make their measurements. And as they worked their way into the foothills of the Himalayas, they saw far off a group of mountain peaks wreathed in cloud.

The survey party never got closer than 150 kilometres. Yet they had no doubt that these were the highest mountains they had ever seen. Excitedly, they took their measurements. They could hardly believe their eyes, but it was true. The highest mountain was over 8800 metres high.

The surveyors questioned the local people, who told them the Tibetan names for the mountains – Changtse, Khumbutse, Nuptse, Lhotse and, greatest of them all, Chomolungma 'the Goddess Mother of the World'.

At first the new mountain was known simply as Peak XV, but in 1863 it was given the name Mount Everest. Its height was thought to be 8840 metres, but later measurements showed that it was in fact 29,028 feet or 8848 metres – unquestionably the

A Piccolo Explorer Book

CONQUERORS OF EVEREST

Brian Williams

Designed by Kate Penoyre

Illustrators
Nigel Chamberlain · Francis Phillips

Pan Books · London and Sydney

TIBET

NEPAL—

Kathmandu

Everest

The officers of the Great Survey of India mapped Mount Everest in 1849.

highest mountain in the world.

No-one then thought of climbing Everest, for mountaineering had hardly begun. In 1865 Edward Whymper (1840–1911) conquered the Matterhorn (4477 metres) in the Swiss Alps. He went on to explore the Andes Mountains of South America and in 1880 he climbed Chimborazo (6310 metres). Whymper studied the effects of 'mountain sickness' at high altitude and pioneered several mountaineering techniques.

One by one the European peaks were conquered. For a new challenge, climbers began to look eagerly towards the distant Himalayas and the mysterious Chomolungma.

The Challenge

Climbing Everest is difficult and dangerous. The climber must overcome deep snow, crevasses, walls of ice and sheer rock faces. He must face the perils of altitude and hope for a spell of good weather.

Above 6400 metres the thin air makes breathing difficult and each step demands a painful effort. Climbing at such heights, a man quickly becomes exhausted and he finds it hard to think clearly.

During the winter, from November to March, freezing winds howl around Everest. Plumes of snow stream from the summit and avalanches crash down the mountain. In early summer the monsoon winds bring blizzards to the Himalayas. Climbers can only venture on Everest just before or just after the monsoon.

Everest can be approached from the north, by way of Tibet, tackling the mountain by the North East Ridge. But most modern expeditions have taken the southern route through Nepal – a route which leads up the Khumbu Glacier and the Icefall.

Below the valley called the Western Cwm the way is blocked by a gigantic step, 600 metres high. This is the Icefall, a treacherous cascade of ice blocks, constantly shifting to reveal yawning crevasses.

Beyond the Icefall wide snow slopes lead up to the icy wall of the Lhotse Face, and above the wall is the point known as the South Col (7900 metres). The route to the summit lies along the snow crest of the South East Ridge – with a drop of thousands of metres on either side.

North East Ridge

West Sh

Icefall

Summit

South Summit

Lhotse

South East Ridge

South Col

Lhotse Face

South West Face

Nupts[e]

Western Cwm

Khumbu Glacier

The challenge which faces those ambitious enough to pit their skill against the highest mountain in the world.
The 1953 expedition used the southern route via the Icefall. The climb up the South West Face is even more dangerous.

The First Attempts

For many years after the discovery of Everest, neither Tibet nor Nepal would allow foreigners near the mountain. It was not until 1921 that the Dalai Lama, leader of Tibet's Buddhists, agreed to allow a British expedition to Everest. A reconnaissance party was sent out by the Alpine Club and the Royal Geographical Society to see if the mountain could be climbed and to find the best route.

The explorers set out from Darjeeling in northern India, and crossed the mountain passes into Tibet. At first they carried their equipment on ponies and yaks, but as they drew nearer to Mt Everest they hired local porters who were used to high altitude and quickly proved their fine ability. Each porter cheerfully carried a pack weighing more than 30 kilograms while the British struggled to acclimatize their bodies to the thin air.

The northern route lay up the Rongbuk Glacier. Frostbite proved a danger, but three members of the advance party managed to climb to a spur on the shoulder of the mountain. From this spur, which they named the North Col, they could see what seemed a safe route to the summit.

In 1922 the first full-scale Everest expedition, led by Brigadier-General Charles Bruce, left Britain. They were full of confidence, for they planned to use oxygen breathing apparatus to overcome the problems of altitude.

At first all went well. Five camps were set up and climbers got to within 600 metres of the summit. But high winds, cold, frostbite and finally

The early climbers achieved considerable heights with limited equipment.

exhaustion forced them back. Worse still, the monsoon broke while they were still high on the mountain. Heavy snow fell and seven Sherpas were swept to their deaths by an avalanche crashing down from the North Col.

The worsening weather forced the 1922 expedition to give up and return home. The tragic end to the attempt had shown that Everest was not to be conquered easily.

The Mystery of 1924

Hopes remained high that Everest could be climbed, and several members of the 1922 expedition were among the British party which challenged the mountain again in 1924. They were confident that, with the help of oxygen, climbers would be able to ascend from the North Col to the summit by way of the North East Ridge. All they needed was a spell of settled weather.

Sadly, ill luck dogged the 1924 expedition. The leader, Brigadier-General Bruce, was taken ill and had to return. The weather was cruel, and wind and snow were so bad that at one point the whole party had to come down the mountain, abandoning the higher camps.

They struggled up once more to the

The fate of Mallory and Irvine is one of the great mysteries of mountaineering.

North Col and managed to set up camps 5 and 6 above it. The climbers were amazed to see choughs (birds belonging to the crow family) even at this great height.

The route along the North East Ridge proved more difficult than had been thought. There were two steep 'steps' that were very dangerous. To avoid this obstacle, the expedition's new leader, Major E. F. Norton, with Hugh Somervell, made a traverse out across the North Face, gaining height as they went. When Somervell became too ill to go on, Norton struggled alone to reach 8560 metres (a height not surpassed until 1952). Somervell later wrote of his feelings: 'One seemed to be above everything in the world and to have a glimpse almost of a god's view of things.'

The next pair to try for the summit were George Leigh Mallory and Andrew Irvine. Mallory was 36 and had been on both the 1921 and 1922 expeditions. Irvine was only 22; it was his first time on Everest.

On June 8 the two set out from Camp 6. Watching from lower down the mountain, N. E. Odell spotted the tiny figures high above. When he lost sight of them in the mist, they were plodding slowly upwards towards the summit. Odell judged that they were some 200 metres from the top. He climbed up to Camp 6 and waited. But there was no sign of Mallory and Irvine. They were never seen again.

Could they have reached the summit? It seems unlikely. Nine years later an ice axe belonging to Mallory was found below the North East Ridge. Probably the two men became exhausted and fell to their deaths from the Ridge. But no-one will ever know.

The Struggle Continues

Despite the tragic end to the 1924 expedition, the British persisted in trying to conquer Everest. The route up to the North Col was reasonably simple; but the last stretch, with its forbidding rock steps, was a hazardous challenge.

The 1933 Everest expedition was led by Hugh Ruttledge. V. Wyn Harris and L. R. Wager were 20 metres below the North East Ridge when they found Mallory's ice axe.

The second rock step barred their way and Wyn Harris and Wager were forced to make a traverse, edging sideways across the couloir (gorge) beneath the summit. Eric Shipton and Frank Smythe reached the same height of about 8560 metres before sickness and worsening snow brought the expedition to an end.

In April 1933 the British finally saw the summit of Everest – but only from an aeroplane. Two specially modified Westlands climbed to 10,700 metres and flew over Everest at a height of only 30 metres. This resulted in the first close-up photographs of the summit of the mountain.

In 1934 a climber called Maurice Wilson attempted the impossible in trying to conquer Everest alone and was killed. His body was found by British mountaineers the next year. They also found footprints, said by the Sherpas to be those of the yeti. Monks in a local monastery claimed to possess the scalp of a yeti. However, scientists think the footprints were more likely those of a bear, while the yeti scalp proved to be the dried skin of a mountain antelope called a serow.

Below: the Sherpas claimed that the footprints belonged to the mysterious yeti.

The 1936 Everest expedition, again led by Hugh Ruttledge, was foiled by an early monsoon which brought heavy snow.

Another British party led by H. W. Tilman tackled Everest in 1938. It was a small expedition with only seven climbers and, unlike the two previous expeditions, Tilman's team used oxygen breathing apparatus. Camp 6 was set up at 8300 metres but deep powder snow made progress difficult. The oxygen equipment proved its worth, but once again bad weather forced the expedition to give up. Everest remained unconquered.

The aerial photographs taken on the first flight over Everest provided valuable information about the summit.

Crossing a crevasse

The Equipment

19th century mountaineers had little climbing equipment, other than ropes and alpenstocks (sturdy poles tipped with an iron point or hook). They relied on natural foot and handholds, although some early climbers did wear climbing irons or crampons on their feet to help grip icy slopes.

As mountaineering techniques improved, climbing aids were developed. These included ice hammers, ice axes, pitons and karabiners or snap-links. By hammering pitons into the rock and fastening rope slings to them by means of snap-links, a modern climber can become a 'human fly' and climb a sheer rock face.

By acclimatizing his body gradually to the thin mountain air, a man can climb to great heights without oxygen. But he cannot carry heavy loads and lack of oxygen causes exhaustion and sickness (Most Everest climbers suffer from coughs, headaches and sore throats even when otherwise fit.) Oxygen bottles are an extra load to

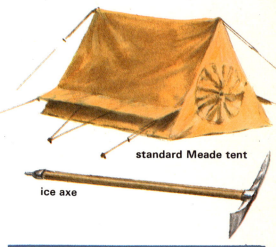
standard Meade tent

ice axe

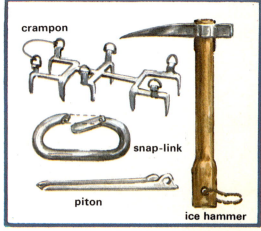
crampon

snap-link

piton

ice hammer

oxygen pack

carry, but they provide vital energy for the final effort.

The climber's equipment must weigh as little as possible. For protection against cold and frostbite, climbers need windproof clothing, with special insulated gloves and boots and sun goggles for their eyes.

Apart from tents, oxygen apparatus, ice axes, crampons, pitons, goggles and so on, an Everest expedition must carry ladders to cross crevasses in the Icefall. The widest crevasses need three special 2-metre ladder sections to bridge them.

While carrying out any tricky manoeuvre, such as crossing a crevasse, a climber is 'belayed' by his companions. If he slips, he is held safely by his rope, which the others have wound round ice axes firmly driven into the snow.

The early attempts on Everest did not fail because the climbers lacked skill or courage. They failed because the final summit teams were inadequately supported. Too much was asked of the climbers and they became exhausted.

Mountaineers realized that they must plan more carefully than ever before. Success on Everest depended on choosing the right equipment, on efficient organization of stores, and on making sure that each camp was kept properly supplied. Then, if the weather held, an expedition should be able to send up the mountain men fit and strong enough to reach the summit itself.

1953: The Plan

World War II prevented further Himalayan expeditions and after 1949 the Chinese occupation of Tibet stopped mountaineers from returning to the route used in the 1920s and 1930s.

However, Nepal now opened its frontiers and in 1951 the British surveyed a new southern route up the Khumbu Glacier. Among the mountaineers was a young New Zealand beekeeper, Edmund Hillary.

In 1952 a Swiss expedition overcame the Icefall and made their way up the Western Cwm to the Lhotse Face and on to the South Col. The sirdar (leader) of the Sherpas was Tenzing Norgay. With the Swiss climber, Raymond Lambert, Tenzing reached a record height of 8600 metres before bad weather forced the Swiss to return to Base.

Spurred on by this near-success, the British organized a new expedition in 1953. They trained in the Himalayas with improved oxygen equipment and planned their assault with great care. The expedition leader was Colonel John Hunt, and among the party he chose were Edmund Hillary and Tenzing Norgay.

Two types of oxygen apparatus were taken to Everest; open-circuit and closed-circuit. Open-circuit provided the climber with a mixture of ordinary air and oxygen. With closed-circuit, he breathed pure oxygen, some of which was recycled and breathed again, making a cylinder last longer.

A team of 350 bearers carried the expedition's stores and equipment from Kathmandu, the capital of

Important selection and training took place at Thyangboche.

Nepal, to Thyangboche. This beautiful spot, 3660 metres up, with its ancient Buddhist monastery, was to be the expedition's first major camp.

From the 35 Sherpas who were to work at high altitude, six including Tenzing, would be chosen to climb with the assault teams. At the age of 39, he had already climbed on Everest six times.

The climbers left Thyangboche in April 1953 to spend three weeks training in the mountains nearby. Then work began on hauling stores up towards the Khumbu Icefall to establish a Base Camp, and later Camps 2 and 3. Here the real difficulties began.

The Assault

As they scrambled up through the Khumbu Icefall, the climbers marked the route with flags. Often these flags vanished overnight as the huge ice blocks shifted and yet another crevasse opened up. Many crevasses were too wide to jump across and were bridged by portable metal ladders. Climbers and Sherpas would then crawl over on their hands and knees.

Crampons and ice axes were essential, and often the weary porters needed handlines to help them clamber up among the ice boulders. Fortunately the going became less hazardous as they moved up the Western Cwm.

Throughout May groups of climbers toiled from one camp to the next, bringing up supplies and equipment. Camps 4 and 5 were pitched on the

The 1953 route. The long Western Cwm led to the Ice-fall and the Lhotse Face. Beyond rose the South Col and the South East Ridge.

Cwm; while 6 and 7 were established on the steep Lhotse Face. There they uncovered the remains of wind-tattered tents, oxygen cylinders and tinned food left by the Swiss.

Below the Lhotse Face the expedition used large pyramid tents. But at the higher camps the men slept in two-man ridge tents. Each tent could be linked to the next by its sleeve entrance.

Each man wore a cotton and nylon windproof suit over a down jacket, three pairs of gloves and special high altitude boots lined with kapok and kept dry by a waterproof outer cover.

Snug inside their sleeping bags, the climbers cooked their meals over primus or butane gas stoves. A typical Everest dinner was a mug of soup, tinned steak and kidney pie, and fruit cake, washed down with tea, coffee or lemonade.

The assault parties moved steadily up from Camp 4 which was at 6470 metres and was also referred to as Advance Base Camp. They worked their way up to the South Col – a three day climb by way of Camps 5, 6 and 7. Beyond Camp 8 on the South Col there was to be a final assault camp, Camp 9, at a height of 8500 metres on the South East Ridge.

The climbers chosen to make the first attempt on the summit were Tom Bourdillon and Charles Evans. Using closed-circuit breathing apparatus, they would start from the South Col. The second pair, Hillary and Tenzing, would be using the open-circuit system and would have to spend a night at Camp 9, high on the Ridge itself. There they would change their oxygen bottles before their attempt on the summit.

The weather was fine although the wind was unrelenting. On May 26 Bourdillon and Evans climbed to the South Summit – higher than any men before them. But it was too late to risk going further, for their start had been delayed by trouble with the oxygen apparatus. Reluctantly, they turned back. Now it was up to Hillary and Tenzing.

Bourdillon and Evans were forced to give up their summit attempt. Next came Hillary and Tenzing. The tiny assault tent pitched below the summit was cramped and uncomfortable, but the view across the Himalayas was breathtaking.

The Triumph

On May 28, 1953 Hillary and Tenzing moved up to Camp 9. Already they were firm friends. Hillary (33) had learned to climb in the New Zealand Alps and Tenzing (39) had run away from his Nepalese village home to become a mountaineer.

They spent an uncomfortable night, for the wind was so fierce that Hillary had to brace his feet against the ridge to stop the tent from being blown away. At 6.30 on May 29, after a breakfast of sardines, biscuits and lemon juice, they set off.

Hillary led the way along the ridge to the South Summit. Beyond lay the final curving crest on which no man had yet set foot. To the right huge snow banks overhung a sheer drop; below the slope on the left was the great rock wall rising from the Western Cwm far below them.

Cutting steps with their ice axes, Hillary and Tenzing plodded upwards. Forced to skirt round a rock, they struggled up through a crevice. This last obstacle passed, Hillary cut a few more steps – and saw the ridge fall away in front of him. They had reached the summit. It was 11.30

For 15 minutes Hillary and Tenzing stood on top of the world. Hillary photographed the incredible view. Tenzing left chocolate, biscuits and sweets as an offering to the gods. As he posed, grinning, for Hillary's camera, the flags of the United Nations, Britain, Nepal and India fluttered from Tenzing's ice axe.

On their weary return to the South Col, they were met by their support team and soon the news was radioed all over the world. The abbot at Thyangboche heard the news in polite disbelief and congratulated Hillary and Tenzing on 'nearly reaching the summit of Chomolungma'.

Everest Yields

1953 was not the end of the Everest story. In 1956 four members of a Swiss party reached the summit by the route through the Khumbu Icefall. In 1960 a Chinese expedition announced that it had climbed Everest by way of the famed North East Ridge. Their claim was disputed by Indian climbers who made an attempt on the summit (by the 1953 route) on the same day as the Chinese. The Indians were forced back by bad weather.

In 1963 a massive American expedition tackled the mountain. One of the aims was to study the effects of high altitude stress for the United States space programme. Eight climbers (including Tenzing's nephew) reached the summit, two of them by a new route up the West Ridge.

The Indians, thwarted a second time in 1962, finally conquered Everest in 1965. In 1970 a Japanese expedition, which included the first woman to challenge the mountain, climbed Everest via the South Col.

Five expeditions were defeated by the South West Face before this difficult and dangerous route was scaled by a British expedition, led by Chris Bonington, in 1975. Before reaching the top, Dougal Haston and Doug Scott spent the night in a tiny bivouac on the South Summit itself.

Recent Everest expeditions have followed the pattern set in 1953. Every detail of the assault is carefully worked out in advance. The 1975 South West Face expedition used a computer to help draw up their plans. Yet even this could not prevent tragedy. For climber Mike Burke was killed while trying

Four successful Everest routes. The Chinese route (shown in red) climbed the North East Ridge. The Americans conquered the West Ridge (green), while the Japanese took a new route via the Lhotse Face and South Col (orange). The British (blue) scaled the treacherous ice wall of the South West Face (right).

to reach the summit on his own after oxygen failure forced his partner to give up.

In 1975 the first all woman team, from Japan, climbed Everest. In 1978 Swiss, Austrian, and German climbers all claimed to have reached the summit without using oxygen for the final assault.

Everest has now been climbed many times but there are still queues of expeditions anxious to test themselves on the mighty 'Goddess Mother of the World'.

The Everest Story

1852	Chomolungma is first mapped
1863	The mountain is named Mount Everest
1921	First reconnaissance expedition, led by Lt-Col C. K. Howard-Bury
1922	First British expedition pioneers North East Ridge route
1924	Norton reaches 8560 metres. Deaths of Mallory and Irvine
1933	Ruttledge's first expedition. First flight over Everest by aircraft of Lady Houston's expedition
1935	Shipton's reconnaissance
1936	Ruttledge's second expedition
1938	Tilman's expedition
1951	Shipton discovers new route to the South Col
1952	Swiss narrowly fail to reach the summit
1953	Triumph of Hillary and Tenzing Norgay
1963	American pair achieve first ascent by the West Ridge, descending by the South Col
1975	First ascent of the South West Face. First ascent by an all-woman expedition

---

THE TOP TEN

The world's highest mountains all lie in the Himalayas, within the lands of Nepal, Sikkim, Tibet or Jammu/Kashmir. Their vital statistics are below.

MOUNTAIN	HEIGHT (in metres)	FIRST ASCENT	DATE
Everest	8848	Britain/Commonwealth	1953
K2	8611	Italy	1954
Kanchenjunga	8595	Britain	1955
Lhotse	8511	Switzerland	1956
Makalu	8481	France	1955
Dhaulagiri	8172	Switzerland	1960
Manaslu	8156	Japan	1956
Cho Oyu	8153	Austria	1954
Nanga Parbat	8126	Austria/Germany	1953
Annapurna	8078	France	1950